MEXICAN GOVERNMENT

Governments Series

Written by Brenda Vance Rollins, Ed. D.

GRADES 5 - 8

Reading Levels 3 - 4

Classroom Complete Press
P.O. Box 19729
San Diego, CA 92159
Tel: 1-800-663-3609 | Fax: 1-800-663-3608
Email: service@classroomcompletepress.com

www.classroomcompletepress.com

ISBN 13: 978-1-55319-345-6

ISBN 10: 1-55319-345-8

 We acknowledge the financial support of the Government of Canada through the Book Publishing Industry Development Program (BPIDP) for our publishing activities. Printed in Canada.

Critical Thinking Skills

Mexican Government

Level	Skills For Critical Thinking	Section 1	Section 2	Section 3	Section 4	Section 5	Section 6	Section 7	Section 8	Writing Tasks
LEVEL 1 Knowledge	• List Facts / Details			✓	✓	✓			✓	✓
	• Recall Information	✓	✓	✓	✓	✓			✓	✓
	• Match	✓	✓		✓	✓	✓	✓	✓	
	• Sequence			✓			✓			
	• Recognize Validity (T/F)		✓	✓	✓	✓		✓	✓	
LEVEL 2 Comprehension	• Compare & Contrast		✓		✓					
	• Summarize	✓		✓	✓	✓				✓
	• State Main Idea			✓		✓		✓		✓
	• Describe		✓	✓		✓	✓	✓	✓	✓
LEVEL 3 Application	• Apply What Is Learned	✓			✓			✓	✓	
	• Infer Outcomes							✓		
LEVEL 4 Analysis	• Draw Conclusions	✓	✓			✓	✓	✓	✓	✓
	• Make Inferences		✓			✓	✓	✓		✓
	• Identify Cause & Effect						✓			✓
LEVEL 5 Synthesis	• Predict					✓		✓		✓
	• Design		✓						✓	✓
	• Create								✓	✓
	• Compile Research		✓	✓	✓	✓	✓	✓	✓	✓
LEVEL 6 Evaluation	• Defend An Opinion							✓		✓
	• Make Judgements					✓		✓		✓

Based on Bloom's Taxonomy

Contents

TEACHER GUIDE

STUDENT HANDOUTS

✔ **6 BONUS Activity Pages! Additional worksheets for your students**

- Go to our website: www.classroomcompletepress.com/**bonus**
- Enter item CC5759
- Enter pass code CC5759D

Assessment Rubric

Mexican Government

Student's Name: ______________________ Assignment: __________________ Level: __________

	Level 1	Level 2	Level 3	Level 4
Understanding Concepts	Demonstrates a limited understanding of the concepts. Requires teacher intervention.	Demonstrates a basic understanding of the concepts.	Demonstrates a good understanding of the concepts.	Demonstrates a thorough understanding of the concepts.
Response to the Text	Expresses responses to the text with limited effectiveness, inconsistently supported by proof from the text	Expresses responses to the text with some effectiveness, supported by some proof from the text	Expresses responses to the text with appropriate skills, supported with appropriate proof	Expresses thorough and complete responses to the text, supported by concise and effective proof from the text
Analysis & Application of Concepts	Interprets and applies various concepts in the text with few, unrelated details and incorrect analysis	Interprets and applies various concepts in the text with some detail, but with some inconsistent analysis	Interprets and applies various concepts in the text with appropriate detail and analysis	Effectively interprets and applies various concepts in the text with consistent, clear and effective detail and analysis

STRENGTHS:

WEAKNESSES:

NEXT STEPS:

Teacher Guide

Our resource has been created for ease of use by both TEACHERS and STUDENTS alike.

Introduction

This resource provides ready-to-use information and activities for remedial students in grades five to eight. Written to grade and using simplified language and vocabulary, social studies concepts are presented in a way that makes them more accessible to students and easier to understand. Comprised of reading passages, student activities and mini posters, our resource can be used effectively for whole-class, small group and independent work.

How Is Our Resource Organized?

STUDENT HANDOUTS

Reading passages and **activities** (*in the form of reproducible worksheets*) make up the majority of our resource. The reading passages present important grade-appropriate information and concepts related to the topic. Embedded in each passage are one or more questions that ensure students understand what they have read.

For each reading passage there are **BEFORE YOU READ** activities and **AFTER YOU READ** activities.

- The BEFORE YOU READ activities prepare students for reading by setting a purpose for reading. They stimulate background knowledge and experience, and guide students to make connections between what they know and what they will learn. Important concepts and vocabulary from the chapters are also presented.
- The AFTER YOU READ activities check students' comprehension of the concepts presented in the reading passage and extend their learning. Students are asked to give thoughtful consideration of the reading passage through creative and evaluative short-answer questions, research, and extension activities.

Writing Tasks are included to further develop students' thinking skills and understanding of the concepts. The **Assessment Rubric** (*page 4*) is a useful tool for evaluating students' responses to many of the activities in our resource. The **Comprehension Quiz** (*page 48*) can be used for either a follow-up review or assessment at the completion of the unit.

PICTURE CUES

This resource contains three main types of pages, each with a different purpose and use. A **Picture Cue** at the top of each page shows, at a glance, what the page is for.

Teacher Guide
- Information and tools for the teacher

Student Handout
- Reproducible worksheets and activities

Easy Marking™ Answer Key
- Answers for student activities

EASY MARKING™ ANSWER KEY

Marking students' worksheets is fast and easy with this **Answer Key**. Answers are listed in columns – just line up the column with its corresponding worksheet, as shown, and see how every question matches up with its answer!

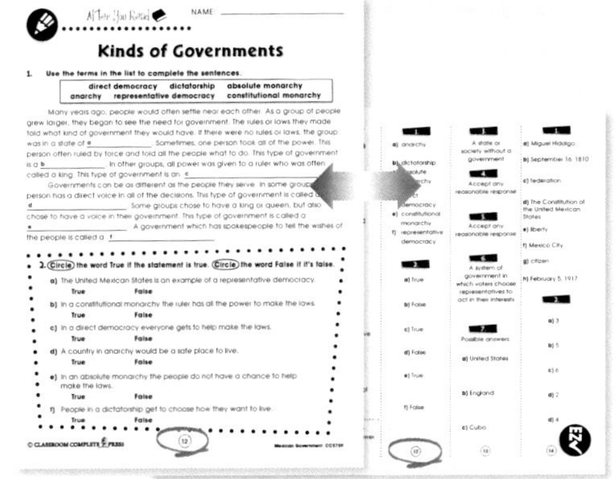

Every question matches up with its answer!

Bloom's Taxonomy

Our resource is an effective tool for any **SOCIAL STUDIES PROGRAM.**

Bloom's Taxonomy* for Reading Comprehension

The activities in our resource engage and build the full range of thinking skills that are essential for students' reading comprehension and understanding of important social studies concepts. Based on the six levels of thinking in Bloom's Taxonomy, and using language at a remedial level, information and questions are given that challenge students to not only recall what they have read, but move beyond this to understand the text and concepts through higher-order thinking. By using higher-order skills of application, analysis, synthesis and evaluation, students become active readers, drawing more meaning from the text, attaining a greater understanding of concepts, and applying and extending their learning in more sophisticated ways.

Our resource, therefore, is an effective tool for any Social Studies program. Whether it is used in whole or in part, or adapted to meet individual student needs, our resource provides teachers with essential information and questions to ask, inspiring students' interest, creativity, and promoting meaningful learning.

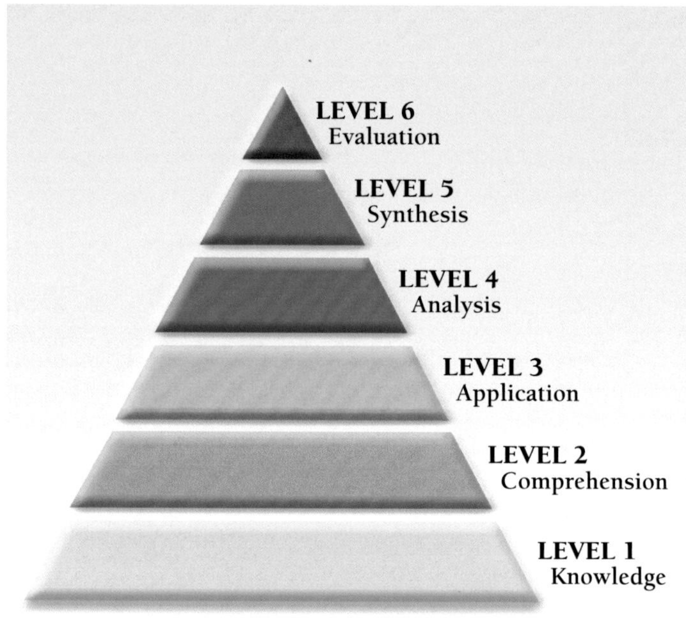

BLOOM'S TAXONOMY:
6 LEVELS OF THINKING

**Bloom's Taxonomy is a widely used tool by educators for classifying learning objectives, and is based on the work of Benjamin Bloom.*

Vocabulary

• rights • authority • enforce • legislate • conflicts • common good • citizens • protect • secure • consent • dictatorship • anarchy • absolute • monarchy • democracy • constitutional • representative • federation • liberty • independence • revolution • colony • sovereign • privileges • chamber • judicial • executive • legislative • congress • senate • justices • supreme court • jury • certify • impeach • amnesty • pardon • conserve • natural resources • agriculture • pollution • crop • economy • decree • amendment • publish • reject • ratify • sponsor • veto • propose • debate • candidate • election • campaign • political party • consecutive • popular vote

NAME: ______________________________

What Is Government?

1. Choose the correct word from the list below to fill each blank. You may use your dictionary to help you.

rights	government	power	authority	enforce	legislate	leader	defend

a) A ____________________ is the person or group of people who makes the rules or laws for everyone else in the country.

b) A ____________________ is one who is in charge or in command of other people.

c) ________________ are anything due to a person or government by law, tradition, or nature.

d) ____________________ means to create or pass laws.

e) ____________________ is the power that people have the right to use because of custom, law, or consent of those being governed.

f) To __________________ something, you keep it safe from danger, attack, or harm.

g) ____________________ is the ability to control someone or something.

h) To __________________ a law means to command obedience to it.

2. Circle the word True if the statement is true. Circle the word False if it's false.

a) A system of government is necessary to keep order in society.

True **False**

b) A system of government is not necessary to protect its citizens' rights.

True **False**

c) People and countries sometimes have conflicts with each other.

True **False**

d) A leader of a country should not be concerned with the common good of its citizens

True **False**

e) The government of a country has the authority to make rules for everyone else.

True **False**

NAME: ______________________________

What Is Government?

There are about 200 different nations in the world. Each one has some form of government. The **government** of a country is the person or group of people who make the rules or laws for everyone else. This person or group has the power or **authority** to make laws. Every country also has a **leader** or leaders who take charge and make plans for it and its people. In most countries, leaders are chosen by the people. However, in some countries leaders use force to take charge of the government. There are many different types of governments in the world.

The care of human life and happiness, and not their destruction, is the first and only object of good government.

Why Do We Need Governments?

What would happen if you and your friends were playing a game that had no rules? Each person could do or say whatever they wished. One player could take all the game pieces or even hurt everyone else. Without rules there would be no consequences. Now think about a country with no rules. This isn't a very pleasant thought, is it? Government is **necessary** to protect the **citizens** and their **rights** or privileges that are due them.

A government should **protect** or keep its citizens safe. A government that provides safety and well-being for its citizens is looking out for their **common good**. Members of a government should **legislate** or make and **enforce** laws to make sure that the people are treated fairly and with dignity.

The governments of two or more countries may have **conflicts** or disagreements. Sometimes these disagreements are so serious that they lead to war between the countries.

STOP

What do you think? Why does a country need laws? Name three laws that you would make if you were the government of a country.

____

____

____

NAME: ______________________________

What Is Government?

1. Fill in each blank with a term from the list. Some terms will be left over.

rights	**leader**	**power**	**authority**	**legislate**	**enforce**
protects	**government**	**secure**	**conflicts**	**consent**	**common good**

a) If you were forming a new country, one of your first jobs would be to make sure that all the people were safe and ____________________.

b) A person or group of people who make the rules for everyone else in a country are called the ____________________.

c) Governments provide a system of rules or laws for people to follow when they have disagreements or ______________________ with each other.

d) The person with the most power in the government is called the country's ____________________.

e) The government should work for the well-being or ______________ __________ of all of its citizens.

f) Often the army ____________________ or keeps the other citizens from danger.

2. Suppose that you are asked to create a new country. What would you name it? What would be the first three laws that you believe should be passed?

____

____

____

3. Sometimes two or more countries disagree so strongly that they begin to wage war against each other. What does "waging war" mean? Do you think that war should be the first solution that the leaders of countries try? Why or why not?

____

____

____

Before You Read

NAME: ______________________

Kinds of Governments

1. Use a straight line to match each word to its meaning. Use a dictionary to help.

dictatorship	Exists when a country has no government at all	A
anarchy	Form of government with a ruler who inherits the position, rules for life, and holds all power	B
absolute monarchy	A government where the highest power is held by all the people and is used by them directly	C
direct democracy	Form of government where all power is held by one person who may use force	D
constitutional monarchy	A government in which voters choose who represents them	E
representative democracy	A government in which the power of the ruler or monarch is limited by law	F

2. Which kind of government does each statement describe? Write its name in the blank. Use the terms in Question 1 above.

a) In this kind of government all the ruling power is held by one person, usually a king or queen.

b) All citizens take part in making the laws in this kind of government.

c) Voters choose representatives to act in their interests in this type of government.

d) This kind of government exists when a leader rules with absolute power, usually by force.

e) This type of government exists when a nation has no person or group in charge, and people can do anything they wish.

f) This kind of government is led by a monarch whose power is limited by law.

NAME: ______________________________

Kinds of Governments

As you learn about the different countries of the world you will find that each one has some kind of government. The government of a country is the person or group of people who make the rules or laws for everyone else. There are many different kinds of governments in the world.

Almost all governments set limits for their citizens. They do this to protect the people's rights and safety. If there were no government, the people could say or do anything they wished. When this happens, the country is in a state of **anarchy**.

One purpose for a country's laws is to tell how much power the ruler or leader has. Another is to insure that all the citizens are treated in a fair and respectful manner.

What do you think? An anarchy allows people to do or say anything they like. Is this a good situation? Why or why not?

____

____

There are over 200 different countries in the world. Many of them do not have the same kinds of government. Some of the main types of governments are:

GOVERNMENT	HOW IT WORKS
Absolute monarchy	- Total rule by one person who makes all the laws for all the people - Usually, the ruler is called a king or queen - Only a few nations in the world have absolute monarchies
Constitutional monarchy	- A form of government where the power of the ruler or monarch is limited by law - The government is usually made up of representatives elected by the people - There are many constitutional monarchies today
Dictatorship	- A country whose leader rules with absolute power, usually by force - Some dictatorships still exist today
Direct democracy	- A system of government in which all the citizens take part in suggesting and making the laws - The ancient city-state of Athens in Greece is a good example of a direct democracy
Representative democracy	- A system of government in which voters choose representatives to act in their interests - The United States is an example of a modern representative democracy
Anarchy	- Exists when there is no government present in a country - The people can do or say anything they wish to anyone

After You Read

NAME: ______________________

Kinds of Governments

1. Use the terms in the list to complete the sentences.

direct democracy	dictatorship	absolute monarchy
anarchy	representative democracy	constitutional monarchy

Many years ago, people would often settle near each other. As a group of people grew larger, they began to see the need for government. The rules or laws they made told what kind of government they would have. If there were no rules or laws, the group was in a state of a ______________. Sometimes, one person took all of the power. This person often ruled by force and told all the people what to do. This type of government is a b ______________. In other groups, all power was given to a ruler who was often called a king. This type of government is an c ______________________.

Governments can be as different as the people they serve. In some groups, every person has a direct voice in all of the decisions. This type of government is called a d ______________________. Some groups chose to have a king or queen, but also chose to have a voice in their government. This type of government is called a e ______________________. A government which has spokespeople to tell the wishes of the people is called a f ______________________.

2. Circle the word True if the statement is true. Circle the word False if it's false.

a) The United Mexican States is an example of a representative democracy.
True **False**

b) In a constitutional monarchy the ruler has all the power to make the laws.
True **False**

c) In a direct democracy everyone gets to help make the laws.
True **False**

d) A country in anarchy would be a safe place to live.
True **False**

e) In an absolute monarchy the people do not have a chance to help make the laws.
True **False**

f) People in a dictatorship get to choose how they want to live.
True **False**

NAME: ______________________

Kinds of Governments

Answer each question with a complete sentence.

3. Write the dictionary's definition of **anarchy**.

____

4. Which do you think would be a better kind of government – an **absolute monarchy** or a **constitutional monarchy**? Explain your opinion.

____

5. If you were designing a government, how important do you think the **rights** of each person should be?

____

6. Write a brief description of a **representative democracy**.

____

____

7. **Become a Research Detective!**
Use an encyclopedia or the Internet to find the answers to these questions.

a) Name one country whose government is a **representative democracy**.

____

b) Name one country that is a **constitutional monarchy**.

____

c) A few countries are still **dictatorships**. Find the name of one of them.

____

NAME: ______________________________

The Constitution of Mexico

1. Complete each sentence with a word from the list. You may use a dictionary, an encyclopedia or the Internet to help you.

The Constitution of the United Mexican States	**federation**	**Mexico City**
February 5, 1917 **Miguel Hidalgo**	**citizen** **liberty**	**September 16, 1810**

a) ______________ ________________ was the Mexican priest who began a revolt against the Spanish government.

b) Mexican Independence Day is celebrated on ______________________.

c) The Mexican states are called a __________________ because each one is equal and controls its own internal affairs.

d) The official name for the supreme law of Mexico is ________________________ ____.

e) Another word for freedom is ________________________________.

f) The national capital of the United Mexican States is ____________________.

g) A person who has rights within a government is called a _________________.

h) The current Mexican Constitution was signed on _________________________.

2. Mexico has had six constitutions during its history. Put them in the correct order from 1 to 6.

_____ **a)** Constitution of 1824

_____ **b)** Constitution of 1857

_____ **c)** Constitution of 1917

_____ **d)** Constitution of 1821

_____ **e)** Constitution of 1835

_____ **f)** Constitution of 1814

NAME: ______________________

The Constitution of Mexico

Mexican history is filled with its struggles for **independence**. Throughout these battles, or revolutions, Mexicans have worked to make their country strong. From the time of its discovery in 1519 until 1821, Mexico was a **colony** of the absolute monarchy of Spain. Spain directly controlled Mexico in every area of life.

A priest named **Miguel Hidalgo** led a revolt against the Spanish rule on September 16, 1810. This date is celebrated as **Mexico's National Independence Day**. Later, in 1821, the first independent Mexican government was formed.

There have been six constitutions in Mexican history. The latest one was signed on February 5, 1917. This day is also remembered as a national holiday. To Mexican citizens, the Constitution of 1917 is the most important set of laws ever made.

What Is the Constitution?

The official name of Mexico's Constitution is the **Political Constitution of the United Mexican States of 1917**. It outlines the rights and responsibilities each citizen has and describes how the government should be run.

The Constitution divides the country into 31 separate and **sovereign states** along with a Federal District, and the Mexican Islands. The **Federal District** is a territory that belongs to all of the states. **Mexico City**, the nation's capital, is in the Federal District. The group of states which form the United Mexican States is called a **federation**. This means that the states are separate and equal with each one controlling its own internal affairs.

The Constitution of 1917 was the result of seven years of fierce fighting. The fighting was about rights and equality among the citizens of Mexico. During this time, over one million people died in the violence. The Constitution was written to describe the rights and privileges all citizens should have no matter how rich or poor they are.

NAME: ______________________

The Constitution of Mexico

What do you think? The Constitution of 1917 was written after nearly seven years of fierce fighting among groups of Mexicans. What were these groups of people fighting about?

____

____

What Does the Constitution Say?

The Constitution is divided into sections called **Titles**. Each Title describes a part of the government and the rights granted to Mexican citizens. The government of Mexico is a **representative democracy** in which the president is both the **head of state** and the **head of the government**.

The government is divided into three parts or **branches**. The president is the leader of the **Executive Branch**. The Constitution of 1917 states that the president can only be elected for one six-year term. There is no vice-president. The president is the supreme commander of the Army, the Navy, and the Air Force. The president's advisors are called **Secretaries of State**. Each one oversees a different area of the government. The most important job of the members of the executive branch is to make sure that the country is governed according to the laws of the Constitution.

The second branch of the Mexican government is the **Legislative Branch**. This branch makes the laws, discusses the country's problems, and oversees the actions of the other branches. The **Legislative Branch** for the whole country is called the **Congress of the Union**. It is made up of the **Chamber of Deputies** and the **Chamber of the Senate**. The job of the members of both groups is to discuss and pass laws that the country needs.

The **Judicial Branch** is in charge of making sure that the Constitution is enforced. Members of this branch also help to resolve conflicts among the citizens of the country. This branch is made up of the **Supreme Court of Justice of the Nation**, the **Electoral Tribunal**, the **Collegiate Tribunals**, the **Unit Circuit Tribunals**, the **District Courts**, and the **Council of the Federal Judicature**.

NAME: ______________________________

The Constitution of Mexico

1. Circle the word True if the statement is true. Circle the word False if it's false. If it is false, rewrite the statement to make it correct.

a) In its early years, Mexico was a colony of France.

True **False** ______________________________

b) Mexicans celebrate their Independence Day on July 4.

True **False** ______________________________

c) The Mexican government is divided into three parts or branches.

True **False** ______________________________

d) The president's advisors are called Secretaries of State.

True **False** ______________________________

2. Write each word or group of words beside the statement that describes it.

Miguel Hidalgo	Titles	federation	Mexico City

[ ] **a)** The national capital of Mexico

[ ] **b)** States are separate and equal with each one controlling its own internal affairs

[ ] **c)** Led a revolt against the Spanish rule on September 16, 1810

[ ] **d)** Sections of the Mexican Constitution

After You Read

NAME: ____________________

The Constitution of Mexico

Answer each question with a complete sentence.

3. The history of Mexico is filled with revolutions and fighting. In most of the battles, what were the Mexicans trying to gain? Why do you think they fought so hard for this goal?

____

____

4. What is the purpose of the Constitution of 1917?

____

5. What had happened in Mexico in the seven years before the Constitution of 1917 was written?

____

____

6. What are the three branches of the Mexican government? What job does each branch do?

____

____

7. Become a Research Detective!

Use an encyclopedia or the Internet to help you find the answers to the following:

Washington, D.C. and Mexico City are both national capitals located in a federal district. Lean more about the two cities by comparing their:

- **country names**
- **populations**
- **areas**
- **monetary units (money)**
- **languages**
- **climate**

Record your answers in the chart on the next page.

NAME: ______________________________

Comparison Chart

Capital City	Washington D.C.	Mexico City
Name of Country		
Monetary Unit (Money)		
Population		
Languages		
Area		
Climate		

NAME: ____________________

Series of Events Chain

Use your knowledge of Mexican history to list and describe four events that led to the Constitution of 1917.

Event 1

↓

Event 2

↓

Event 3

↓

Event 4

Three Branches of the Mexican Government

1. **Fill in each blank with the correct term from the list. You may use a dictionary if you wish. Some terms will be used more than once.**

president	judicial	executive	legislative	Senate
Chamber of Deputies	sexenio	Justices		

a) The three branches of the Mexican government are the ______________ branch, the ______________ branch, and the ______________ branch.

b) The Chamber of Deputies and the Senate are the divisions of the ______________.

c) The chief executive of the United Mexican States is called the ______________.

d) Another name for Supreme Court judges is Supreme Court ______________.

e) The branch of government which makes sure the laws of the land are followed is called the ______________ branch.

f) The branch of government that makes sure the Constitution of 1917 is followed is called the ______________ branch.

g) The branch of government that makes laws is called the ______________ branch.

h) The President of Mexico serves only one six-year term called a ______________.

NAME: ____________________

Three Branches of the Mexican Government

The authors of the Constitution of 1917 decided that a government divided into three parts would be much fairer than a government with just one part. They did not want one person or group to hold all the power. This idea is called **separation of powers**. They gave the new Mexican government three branches. Each one would have its own jobs and responsibilities.

The branches of the government of the United Mexican States are: the **legislative**, **executive**, and **judicial**. The Constitution of 1917 describes the duties that each branch has and the titles of the people who carry out these duties. Each branch must follow the Constitution of 1917 at all times. The headquarters for each branch of government is in Mexico City, D.F. ("Distrito Federal"), the nation's capital.

The **Executive Branch** makes sure that the laws of the country are obeyed and that the Constitution of 1917 is followed. The **President** is the head of the executive branch. **Chapter III** of the Third Title of the **Constitution** describes the duties of the executive branch. There is no vice-president in Mexican government. The president is assisted by his **cabinet**. The cabinet is made up of **18 Secretaries of State**, the head of the federal executive legal office, and the **Attorney General**. The president is elected for one six-year term, called a **sexenio**.

Chapter III of the Third Title of the Mexican Constitution states that, for one to run for President of Mexico, a person must be: 1) a Mexican citizen by birth, with a father and mother who are Mexican by birth, who has resided in the country for at least 20 years; 2) 35 years old, or older, at the time of the election; 3) a resident in the country for the entire year before the election; 4) not an official of any church or religious denomination; 5) not in active military service during the six months before the election; 6) not a secretary or under-secretary of state, attorney general, or governor of a state for at least six months before the election and; 7) never been president already (by election, or other causes).

NAME: ______________________

Three Branches of the Mexican Government

The **judicial branch** answers questions about the meaning of laws and whether or not they follow the Constitution. The highest court in the judicial branch is called the **Supreme Court of Justice of the Nation**. It is made up of a President of the Supreme Court (Chief Justice) and 10 Ministers (Associate Justices). The justices are appointed by the Senate from a list that is proposed by the President of the Republic. The justices serve for 15 years and may not serve a second term. Chapter IV of the Third Title of the Constitution of Mexico describes the powers of the judicial branch.

The legislative branch makes laws for the nation. It is made up of the Congress of the Union and some government agencies. Chapter II of the Third Title of the Constitution of Mexico describes the powers of the **legislative branch**. The Congress of the Union has two parts – the Senate and Chamber of Deputies.

1. Did you know? What are the three branches of the United Mexican States' government called? What are the duties of each branch?

____

____

The powers of the Congress of the Union include the right to: 1) pass laws, 2) impose taxes, 3) declare war, 4) approve the national budget, 5) approve or reject treaties and conventions made with foreign countries, and 6) ratify diplomatic appointments. The Senate answers all questions about foreign policy, approves international agreements, and confirms presidential appointments. The Chamber of Deputies, much like the United States House of Representatives, answers all questions about the government's budget and public spending.

2. Look It Up! Who is the President of the United Mexican States now? When was he elected?

____

____

NAME: ______________________

Three Branches of the Mexican Government

1. Circle the word True if the statement is true. Circle the word False if it's false. If it is false, rewrite the statement to make it correct.

a) The writers of the Constitution of 1917 thought a monarchy would be the best type of government for Mexico.

True **False** ______________________

b) The main goal of the separation of powers is to make sure that no person or group has all the power in the government.

True **False** ______________________

c) It is not important for citizens' rights to be considered in government.

True **False** ______________________

d) The judicial branch makes sure that all laws agree with the Constitution of 1917.

True **False** ______________________

e) The head of the Mexican government is the Chief Justice.

True **False** ______________________

f) The national capital of Mexico is Mexico City, D.F.

True **False** ______________________

g) The Secretaries of State help the justices of the Supreme Court of Justice of the Nation with their duties.

True **False** ______________________

h) The Congress of the Union can declare war on other countries.

True **False** ______________________

i) The legislative branch answers questions about the meaning of laws and whether or not they follow the Constitution.

True **False** ______________________

2. Write a letter! Imagine that you are a child in Mexico who wants the president to help with a problem in your town. Decide what the problem is. Then, write a letter to the President asking for help.

NAME: ______________________________

Three Branches of the Mexican Government

3. **(Circle) F if the statement is FACT (anything that can be proven). (Circle) O if it is OPINION (how someone feels about the subject).**

F O a) The government of the United Mexican States is the best government in the world.

F O b) There are 18 Secretaries of State in the executive branch of the government.

F O c) The president of the United Mexican States made a bad decision about trading with other countries.

F O d) Everyone from age to 2 to 100 should be allowed to vote in Mexico.

F O e) The Justices of the Supreme Court of the Nation serve for 15 years and may not serve a second term.

F O f) The Constitution of 1917 is the best supreme law Mexico has ever had.

F O g) The executive branch is the most important branch of the Mexican government.

F O h) The United Mexican States is made up of 31 states and the federal district.

F O i) Having a government with three branches is the only way to make sure that it is fair to all the citizens.

F O j) Every country's president should have a vice-president to help him.

4. **Become a Research Detective!** Use an encyclopedia or the Internet to answer this question: **How many people live in each Mexican state?**

1. Aguascalientes
2. Baja California
3. Baja California Sur
4. Campeche
5. Chiapas
6. Chihuahua
7. Coshuila
8. Colima
9. Durango
10. Guanajuato
11. Guerrero
12. Hidalgo
13. Jalisco
14. Mexico
15. Michoacan
16. Morelos
17. Nayarit
18. Nuevo Leon
19. Oaxaca
20. Puebla
21. Queretaro
22. Quintaria Roo
23. San Luis Potosi
24. Sinaloa
25. Sonora
26. Tabasco
27. Tamaulipas
28. Tlaxacala
29. Veracruz
30. Yucatan
31. Zacatecas

Before You Read

NAME: ______________________

System of Checks and Balances

1. Write each term beside the correct meaning.

separation of powers	veto	constitutional	executive branch
pardon	legislative branch	judicial branch	resign

- ______ **a)** To stop or end a law
- ______ **b)** Agreeing with the Constitution of 1917
- ______ **c)** A plan in which one branch of a government makes sure that the other branches do not have too much power
- ______ **d)** The President of the Republic, Secretaries of State, the head of the federal executive legal office, and the Attorney General
- ______ **e)** The Supreme Court of Justice of the Nation, district courts, and magistrates
- ______ **f)** The Chamber of Deputies and the Senate
- ______ **g)** To quit or leave office
- ______ **h)** To end or take away a court sentence

2. Fill in the blanks in the diagram below. Use the terms in the box.

Supreme Court of the Justice of the Nation	Chamber of Deputies	President
Secretaries of State	Senate	Federal Executive Legal Office	Attorney General

The Government of the United Mexican States

Executive
1 ______
2 ______
3 ______
4 ______

Legislative
1 ______
2 ______

Judicial
1 ______

NAME: ______________________

System of Checks and Balances

Throughout its history, the citizens of Mexico have fought and died for liberty and independence. The goal of the writers of the Constitution of 1917 was to make sure that no person or branch of government had too much power. This is why they included a **system of checks and balances** in the Constitution. Each branch **checks**, or holds back, the other two. This helps to keep the balance of power even in all three branches.

The Checking Power of the Executive Branch

The president is the head of the executive branch of the government. He can **check** the power of the legislative branch by using his power of **veto** which prevents a bill from becoming a law. Every bill that is approved by the Chamber of Deputies or the Senate is sent to the president for his approval. If he chooses not to approve the law, we say that he has vetoed it.

The president can veto almost any bill sent by Congress. He cannot veto bills where members of Congress **act as a jury** or when they **certify** or **confirm the results of an election**. Having this ability gives the President strong checking power over the legislative branch.

STOP

What Do You Think? Why do you think it is necessary for each branch of the government to have checking powers over the other two branches?

____

____

____

____

NAME: ____________________

System of Checks and Balances

The president can check the power of the judicial branch of the government in several ways. He can:

1. recommend the appointments of the magistrates of the superior court of justice of the Federal District and of the Territories;
2. **pardon**, or forgive, any federal or territorial criminal;
3. grant special privileges to discoverers, inventors, or improvers in any branch of industry and;
4. recommend the removal of any judicial authority due to bad conduct.

The Checking Power of the Legislative Branch

The Constitution of 1917 also gives strong checking powers to the Congress. The **Chamber of Deputies** can check the other two branches by:

1. **impeaching** the president, or putting him on trial, for treason to the country and serious common crimes;
2. granting **amnesties**, or pardons, for crime within the federal court system and;
3. granting or refusing approval for judges of the supreme court.

The **Senate** checks the other two branches by:

1. acting as a grand jury for government officers and;
2. accepting or denying the President's request to remove judges of the court.

The Checking Power of the Judicial Branch

The judicial branch of the Mexican government uses its checking powers to make sure that the laws proposed and passed by the other two branches follow the constitution.

NAME: ______________________________

System of Checks and Balances

1. Circle the word True if the statement is true. Circle the word False if it's false. If it is false, rewrite the statement to make it correct.

a) The president is the head of state and head of the executive branch.

True **False** ______________________________

b) "Veto" means the same as "pardon."

True **False** ______________________________

c) Each branch of the Mexican government checks the other two.

True **False** ______________________________

d) The president of Mexico cannot be impeached.

True **False** ______________________________

e) The judicial branch decides whether laws are constitutional.

True **False** ______________________________

f) The president of Mexico serves a five-year term called a "sexenio".

True **False** ______________________________

g) The Secretaries of State are members of the legislative branch of government.

True **False** ______________________________

2. Become a Research Detective!

Use your encyclopedia or the Internet to find the answer to the following:

Has a woman ever been elected president of Mexico? If so, what is her name?

Are there any women among the secretaries of state in the executive branch? If so, who are they?

____

____

After You Read

NAME: ______________________

System of Checks and Balances

Answer each question with a complete sentence.

3. What is the reason for having a **system of checks and balances** in a government?

____

____

4. Why do you think a person would be willing to fight, and even die, for **freedom**? Do you think that freedom is very important? Why?

____

____

5. Read the presidential oath (promise) below. What are **two** things that the president is promising to do when he takes this oath?

The Mexican Presidential Oath of Office

"I solemnly promise that I will observe and enforce the Political Constitution of the United Mexican States and the laws enacted in pursuance thereof, and that I will discharge loyally and patriotically the office of President of the Republic which the people have conferred upon me, in all ways looking to the welfare and prosperity of the Union; and if I do not do so may the Nation demand it of me."

____

____

6. Describe **two** ways that the executive branch can check the legislative branch.

____

____

7. When is the only time that the president **cannot** veto a law sent to him by the legislative branch?

____

____

NAME: ______________________

Departments of the Executive Branch of Government

1. **Use a dictionary to find the meaning of the words below.**

a) department ______________________

b) conserve ______________________

c) resource ______________________

d) tourism ______________________

e) agriculture ______________________

f) pollution ______________________

g) crops ______________________

2. Choose **four** list words from Question 1 above. Write each word in a complete sentence that shows the meaning of the word.

Word: ______________________

Sentence: ______________________

Word: ______________________

Sentence: ______________________

Word: ______________________

Sentence: ______________________

Word: ______________________

Sentence: ______________________

NAME: ____________________

Departments of the Executive Branch of Government

As you have already learned, there are three branches of the Mexican government: **executive, legislative, and judicial**. The executive branch has the important job of making sure that the laws of the country are obeyed. Remember that the president is the head of the executive branch. This branch is very large because many people are needed to help the president, and there are many jobs to do.

The president names the people who will help him run the country. These people are called **Secretaries of State**. Each Secretary of State is in charge of a specific area, or **department**, of the executive branch of government. Each department has an important job to help run the country well. For example, one department looks after Mexico's health care. Another department looks after **communication** and **transportation**. A third department is in charge of **tourism**. The executive branch is divided into many different departments. Let's look at five of them to find out what each one does.

STOP

Why is the executive branch of government divided into different departments?

____

____

Department of Health

People who work in this department make sure that Mexican citizens have the **medical care** they need. They run special activities and programs to help Mexicans stay healthy, and get the medicines they need if they are sick. Some of these workers also do research on **diseases** and medicines to help fight them.

NAME: ______________________

Departments of the Executive Branch of Government

Department of Communications and Transportation

Mexico's transportation includes many roads, highways, airports, train tracks, train stations and sea ports (for boats along ocean coasts). This department has the job of building these things and making sure they stay in good and strong repair so people can safely use them. Also, it is in charge of mail and telephone systems which are important for communication in Mexico and with other countries.

Department of the Environment, Natural Resources and Fisheries

This department has the important job of taking care of Mexico's natural environments. It protects and **conserves** wildlife and the natural lands and waters where plants and animals live. It makes sure that **natural resources** like forests, soils and seas are used well by businesses and other organizations. It makes sure that Mexico does not run out of these things so that they will be available for use by future generations.

Department of Tourism

People who work for this department help attract visitors to Mexico. Visitors come from all over the world for vacations. This department makes sure that there are healthy and safe places for visitors to stay, and that prices for visitor services are not too high. Tourism is important because it brings money into the country and helps the economy.

Department of Agriculture and Rural Development

This part of the government helps people in rural areas (the countryside) live well. It helps families have work and teaches people about **agriculture**. These citizens learn how to grow rice, corn and beans, for example, using the resources around them. This department also makes sure that the land and water in rural areas stay clean from **pollution**. This way it is safe for people to live and raise healthy animals and **crops**.

After You Read

NAME: ____________________

Departments of the Executive Branch of Government

1. Circle the word True if the statement is true. Circle the word False if it's false.

a) The executive branch of the Mexican government is not very big.

True **False**

b) It is the job of each state to look after the health care of the people who live there.

True **False**

c) Money spent by tourists is important for Mexico's economy.

True **False**

d) It doesn't matter if Mexico's natural resources are all used up.

True **False**

e) Telephone and mail systems are examples of communication in Mexico.

True **False**

f) It is the job of the executive branch of government to help Mexicans who live in rural areas.

True **False**

2. Use a straight line to match the Department with its job.

Tourism		Teaches people how to grow crops	A
Health		Conserves wildlife and their natural environments	B
Agriculture and Rural Development		Researches diseases and medicines	C
Communications and Transportation		Brings visitors to Mexico	D
Environment, Natural Resources and Fisheries		Builds highways and airports	E

NAME: ___________________________

After You Read

Departments of the Executive Branch of Government

Answer each question with a complete sentence.

3. What are two important jobs of the Department of Health?

____

____

4. If a citizen wanted to write a letter about a problem with Mexico's airports, which department would he or she send it to?

____

____

5. Why is it important that the Department of Agriculture and Rural Development make sure that land and water in the countryside is not polluted?

____

____

6. In your opinion, how important is it that the executive branch of government protects the forests, soils and seas of Mexico? Give good reasons for your answer.

____

____

7. Become a Research Detective!
Use an encyclopedia or the Internet to help you find the answers to the following:

Find the names of two more departments in the executive branch of the federal government. Describe the main jobs of each department.

____

____

NAME: ______________________________

How a Bill Becomes a Law

1. Put the correct term in each blank. Use the information in each sentence or a dictionary to help you.

decree	committee	bill	chambers	publish
10 business days	rejected	amendments	ratify	

a) ____________________ is another name for a law.

b) The two sections of the Congress are also called its two ____________________.

c) A ____________________ is a suggestion for a law.

d) The word ____________________ means the same as the word "approve".

e) When a bill is approved, the president will announce it to the public or ____________________ it.

f) After they are introduced, all bills go to a ____________________, or smaller group of legislators to be studied and discussed.

g) When a bill is not approved we can say that it was ____________________.

h) The president must return a bill to the Congress within ____________________ or it is considered approved.

i) Additions to a bill are called ____________________.

2. Use a straight line to match each word to its definition.

sponsor	to suggest	A
veto	discussion	B
propose	a draft of a proposed law	C
debate	one who proposes a law	D
bill	to say no, or forbid the passage of a law	E

NAME: ______________________

How a Bill Becomes a Law

You may have heard someone say, "There ought to be a law..." Thoughts like these are the beginning of the law-making process. Anyone in Mexico may have ideas about the kinds of laws that need to made, but only certain people can suggest them. In Mexico, the right to introduce laws or decrees belongs to: 1) the President of the Republic, 2) the deputies and senators of the Congress, and 3) the legislatures of the States.

As soon as one of these people proposes a bill (a law that has yet to be approved) it is sent directly to a committee for study. This committee is usually made up of a smaller group of legislators and the President's representatives.

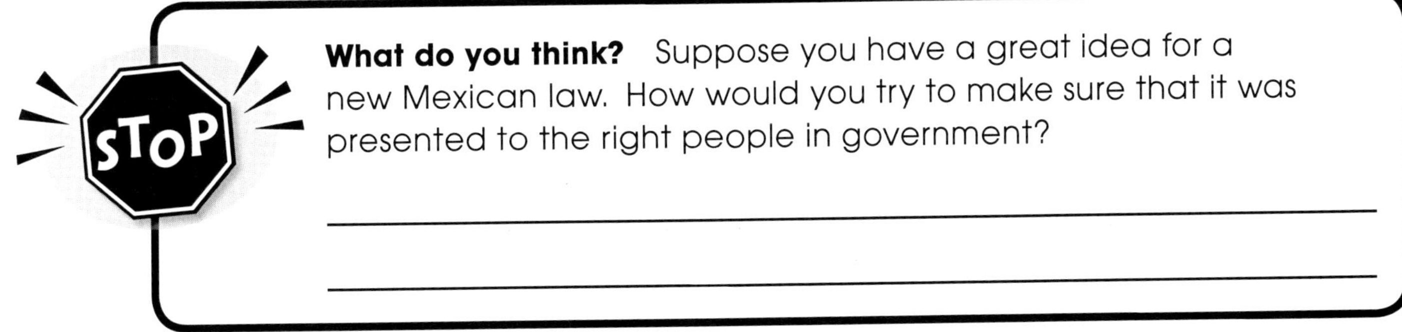

What do you think? Suppose you have a great idea for a new Mexican law. How would you try to make sure that it was presented to the right people in government?

____

____

After the committee has read and discussed the bill, it is presented for a vote in one of the two **chambers**, or sections, of the Congress. If a majority of the members of that chamber approve the bill, it then goes to the other chamber. There it is discussed and voted on. Finally, if the bill is approved in both chambers, it is sent to the president for approval.

The president has the right to approve, or **veto** (disapprove), the bill. He can sign the bill which makes it a law. Or he can do nothing for ten business days and the bill will automatically become a law.

When a bill is approved, the president **publishes**, or announces it to the public. The president can veto or disapprove entire bills or parts of them. He then makes notes about the sections he is vetoing and sends the bill back to the chamber for changes.

If a two-thirds majority of the legislators agree with the changes, the bill is then sent to the other chamber for the same process. If two-thirds of that chamber's members approve the bill, it becomes a law without the president's signature.

After You Read

NAME: ______________________

How a Bill Becomes a Law

1. Circle the word True if the statement is true. Circle the word False if it's false. If it is false, rewrite the statement to make it correct.

   a) Mayors of large Mexican cities can propose bills to the Congress.
      True **False** ______________________

   b) The committee that studies proposed laws is made up of legislators and the president's representatives.
      True **False** ______________________

   c) The Congress of the Union is made up of the Chamber of Deputies and Chamber of the Senate.
      True **False** ______________________

   d) The president does not have the right to veto any bill placed before him.
      True **False** ______________________

   e) When the president publishes a new law, he prints it in a large book and sells it to the citizens.
      True **False** ______________________

   f) The members of state legislatures can propose bills in the Congress of the Union.
      True **False** ______________________

   g) If a bill stays on the president's desk for five days without his signature, it automatically becomes a law.
      True **False** ______________________

2. **Does the president have more power in the law-making process than the Congress? Why or why not?**

____

____

3. **Do you think that the law-making process is a very quick one? Why or why not?**

____

____

How a Bill Becomes a Law

4. Number the events from 1 to 7 in the order they occur.

______ **a)** The president approves the bill or vetoes it (does not approve it).

______ **b)** The bill goes to a smaller group, called a committee, for discussion and debate.

______ **c)** A bill is introduced by a member of Congress, the president, or a member of a state legislature.

______ **d)** The entire chamber votes on the bill.

______ **e)** The committee approves the bill and returns it to the group for a vote.

______ **f)** If the entire group approves the bill, it goes to the other chamber of Congress.

______ **g)** Both sections of Congress approve the bill and send it to the President.

5. Surfing the net! On the Internet, find a website that has a picture of the Mexican flag. It looks like the picture below. What colors are the different parts of the flag? Color the flag below. Be sure to put the correct colors in the right places!

NAME: ______________________

Elections and Political Parties

Write the correct term in each blank. You may use your dictionary if you wish.

candidate	**political party**	**campaign**	**election**
major political parties in the United Mexican States	**six**	**consecutive**	
state governments	**vote**		

Answer		Definition
	A	National Action Party (PAN), Institutional Revolutionary Party (PRI), Party of the Democratic Revolution (PRD), Labor Party, Green Ecological Party of Mexico, Convergence, Social Democratic and Farmer Alternative, and New Alliance
	B	Activities designed to help a person get elected to public office
	C	To select or choose
	D	A group with the same ideas about running the government
	E	A person who wants to hold public office
	F	The time when citizens vote for the candidates of their choice
	G	Generally are set up in the same manner as the federal government
	H	Years in a presidential term
	I	One after the other

Elections and Political Parties

Since the United Mexican States is a **democracy**, all of its government leaders are **elected**, or chosen by the citizens. The Constitution of 1917 states all the requirements for each federal office. These must be fulfilled before a person can run for office. A person who runs for an elected office is called a **candidate**.

The Constitution of 1917 also states the length of terms for each federal office. In Mexico, a person can only be elected president once. The president serves one, six-year term, called a sexenio. Elections for the Chamber of Deputies occur every three years. Deputies cannot serve **consecutive** terms, but may run for office again after three years have passed. A senate term is six years.

What do you think? Why do you think a person would want to run for president or Congress of the Union? Write at least three reasons in complete sentences.

____

____

Political Parties

There are eight major **political parties** in the United Mexican States. Each party is made up of a group of people who share the same kinds of ideas about how the government should be run. The major political parties in Mexico are:

- National Action Party (PAN)
- Institutional Revolutionary Party (PRI)
- Party of the Democratic Revolution (PRD)
- Labor Party
- Green Ecological Party of Mexico
- Convergence
- Social Democratic and Farmer Alternative
- New Alliance

NAME: ____________________

Elections and Political Parties

The **Institutional Revolutionary Party** was the largest party during most of the Twentieth Century. All Mexican presidents elected from 1911 to 1996 were members of this party. The election of Vicente Fox as president in 2000 finally changed the trend. Vicente Fox belonged to the **National Action Party**, the second most popular political party. The six remaining parties have different numbers of followers.

The president of Mexico is elected by **popular vote**. This means that whoever gets the most votes cast by the people is the winner of the election. Members of the Congress of the Union and the governors of the states are elected in the same way.

Why was the election of Vicente Fox important in Mexico's history? How was he elected?

____

____

Getting Elected

Getting elected President of the United Mexican States is very hard to do. It takes lots of money and many supporters to run a campaign for the presidency. Today, running for any office can be costly and time-consuming. People who want to serve in public office must be dedicated and prepared for hard work.

Be In the Know: Use a reference book or the internet to do the following work.

Make a chart of all the presidents of the United Mexican States. Begin with Benito Juarez and end with the present President. Be sure to include the date the person was elected, the dates he or she held office, and the political party of the president.

NAME: ______________________

Elections and Political Parties

1. Circle the word True if the statement is true. Circle the word False if it's false.

a) In a democracy only a few of the government leaders are elected by the citizens.

True **False**

b) A person who was born in the U.S.A. could become President of the United Mexican States.

True **False**

c) A presidential term in the United Mexican States lasts for four years.

True **False**

d) There are five major political parties in Mexico.

True **False**

e) It is not very difficult to run for the presidency of the United Mexican States.

True **False**

2. Write each term beside its meaning.

democracy	**candidate**	**campaign**	**elected**	**popular vote**
major political parties in the United Mexican States			**presidential term**	

a) National Action Party and Institutional Revolutionary Party are examples

b) Votes cast by the people

c) Six years

d) A person who is running for public office

e) Chosen for public office

f) Activities designed to help a person get elected to public office

g) Government by the people

After You Read

NAME: ______________________

Elections and Political Parties

Answer each question with a complete sentence.

3. Describe the process of running for the office of President of the United Mexican States.

4. What **personal qualities** do you think a person should have who wants to be the President of the United Mexican States? Try to think of at least three. Give reasons for your answers.

5. We have read about a number of **major political parties** in Mexico. Choose one of these parties that you would like to learn more about. Research this party to find some interesting facts about it. Use the Internet, an encyclopedia, or books from the library to find your information. If you were a Mexican citizen, would you want to be a member of this party? Why or why not? Write your answers in your notebook.

6. **Use Your Brain!**

What subjects do you think that a person who plans on running for public office should study in college? Why?

Writing Tasks

Here are six writing tasks about the government of Mexico. Be sure to think about all that you have learned about the Mexican government as you write. Write your answers in complete sentences in your notebook.

Task #1 Every country on earth has some kind of government even though all governments are not alike. All governments have leaders. What is the title of the person who leads the Mexican government? How is he or she selected?

Task #2 Being the leader of a large country like Mexico is a very big task for anyone. What kind of qualities do you think the leader of the Mexican government should have? What kind of qualities do you think the leader of your country should have? Compare the qualities you have given for each leader. Give good reasons for your opinion.

Task #3 Article 3 of the Mexican Constitution of 1917 states, "Every individual has the right to receive education." Why do you think the writers of the Constitution thought an education was so important?

Task #4 All countries have problems which must be solved. Some of these problems are so serious that they are present in most countries (for example, homelessness). If you were president of the United Mexican States which three problems would you try to solve? What would you do to solve them?

Task #5 The Mexican president has many powers. Think about what you have learned about the Mexican government and describe three of the powers the Mexican president has. What document gives him these powers?

Task #6 The Constitution of 1917 states that slavery is forbidden in Mexico. What is slavery? What basic rights are taken away from a person who is a slave to another person or group of people?

After You Read

NAME: ____________________

Crossword Puzzle!

Word List		
government	balances	dictator
pardon	conflicts	judicial
executive	candidate	protect
Deputies	Hidalgo	branch
democracy	Senate	power
good	sexenio	anarchy
rights	federation	vote
	Titles	

Down

1. Chamber of the ________
2. to forgive
4. Another word for "might"
5. The common ______
6. An army should ________ the citizens
7. A group of independent states
8. Checks and __________
9. One who has all the power and rules by force
10. The Chamber of ________ ________
12. A person who is running for political office

Across

1. Presidential term in Mexico
3. Person or group of people who make the rules for everyone else
4. Privileges due to a person because he lives in a particular place
5. Sections of the Mexican Constitution
6. Another word for disagreements or battles
7. One division of government
8. Miguel _______, Mexican patriot
10. A form of government in which the people select the ones who govern them
11. In a democracy, a citizen casts his _____ for president
12. The branch of the Mexican government which makes sure that the laws are constitutional
13. Having no government at all
15. Judicial, Legislative and _________

NAME: ______________________________

Word Search

Find all of the words in the Word Search. Words may be horizontal, vertical, or diagonal. A few may even be backwards! Look carefully!

leader	democracy	titles	chambers
citizens	independence	branches	publishes
rights	hidalgo	sexenio	democracy
enforce	sovereign	checks	elected
anarchy	mexico city	veto	political
monarchy	federation	pardon	parties
constitution	president	authority	vote

c	h	e	c	k	s	a	b	s	r	e	b	m	a	h	a	c	d
m	i	l	k	j	t	i	h	g	f	e	r	d	c	b	u	z	y
n	d	o	p	q	h	i	n	o	d	r	a	p	r	s	t	u	v
d	a	c	b	a	g	z	t	y	x	w	n	v	u	t	h	r	q
e	l	f	g	h	i	i	j	l	k	l	c	m	n	b	o	p	q
r	g	s	p	o	r	n	m	l	e	k	h	j	i	h	r	e	a
a	o	e	d	f	g	t	e	w	q	s	e	n	m	u	i	i	n
e	v	i	i	b	o	i	n	e	x	e	s	e	n	e	t	l	s
m	n	t	s	y	t	u	b	v	e	j	q	k	b	e	y	l	i
h	o	r	n	o	e	l	k	r	y	c	a	r	c	o	m	e	d
t	r	a	e	r	v	o	t	e	p	o	r	y	k	r	j	a	w
w	i	p	z	l	m	e	x	i	c	o	c	i	t	y	y	d	c
s	n	v	i	p	e	y	r	d	s	a	q	w	e	h	r	e	o
b	d	e	t	y	q	c	u	e	j	w	b	e	e	c	o	r	n
w	e	g	i	h	j	k	t	s	i	z	x	p	a	r	t	e	s
i	p	e	c	w	q	a	r	e	s	g	d	o	f	a	h	j	t
j	e	c	r	v	b	e	m	y	d	e	n	l	w	n	e	r	i
y	n	f	g	h	b	l	h	x	c	n	m	i	q	o	w	e	t
p	d	q	u	m	r	c	e	r	w	q	m	t	n	m	b	v	u
l	e	w	a	o	r	y	o	t	n	e	d	i	s	e	r	p	t
a	n	h	b	a	j	f	g	d	s	d	s	c	a	q	w	q	i
l	c	a	n	m	n	o	f	e	d	e	r	a	t	i	o	n	o
h	e	a	f	e	f	y	s	e	h	s	i	l	b	u	p	h	n

After You Read

NAME: ______________________

Comprehension Quiz

25

Part A

Circle the word True if the statement is true. Circle the word False if it's false. If it is false, rewrite the statement to make it correct.

1. A government is the person or group who makes the rules for all the other citizens in a country.

True **False** ______________________

2. Governments are not necessary in all countries.

True **False** ______________________

3. Most governments in the Western Hemisphere are monarchies.

True **False** ______________________

4. The Constitution of 1917 was written in order to set up a government for Mexico.

True **False** ______________________

5. In a country with popular sovereignty the citizens hold the highest power in the government.

True **False** ______________________

6. The Institutional Revolutionary Party and the National Action Party are the two most popular political parties in Mexico.

True **False** ______________________

7. The government of the United Mexican States is a representative monarchy.

True **False** ______________________

8. The government of Mexico is divided into four branches.

True **False** ______________________

9. The Mexican president's advisors are called Secretaries of Senate.

True **False** ______________________

10. In Mexico, the right to introduce laws or decrees belongs to the deputies and senators of the Congress only.

True **False** ______________________

SUBTOTAL: /10

NAME: ______________________

After You Read

Comprehension Quiz

Part B

Answer each question in complete sentences.

1. Explain why the framers of the Constitution built a system of **checks and balances** into the three branches of government. 1

____

____

2. Describe the qualifications a person must have to run for **president** of the United Mexican States. 3

____

____

3. In your opinion, what form of government is best for its citizens? Why? 3

____

____

4. Name each **branch** of the Mexican government and tell what each one does. 6

____

____

____

____

____

5. Why is **Miguel Hidalgo** important in Mexican history? 2

____

____

SUBTOTAL: /15

1.

a) government

b) leader

c) rights

d) legislate

e) authority

f) defend

g) power

h) enforce

2.

a) True

b) False

c) True

d) False

e) True

(7)

To keep order. Answers will vary

(8)

1.

a) secure

b) government

c) conflicts

d) leader

e) common good

f) protects

2.

Accept any reasonable answer

3.

Accept any reasonable answer

(9)

1.

dictatorship – **D**

anarchy – **A**

absolute monarchy – **B**

direct democracy – **C**

constitutional monarchy – **F**

representative democracy – **E**

2.

a) absolute monarchy
b) direct democracy
c) representative democracy

d) dictatorship
e) anarchy
f) constitutional monarchy

(10)

Accept any reasonable answer

(11)

1.

a) anarchy

b) dictatorship
c) absolute monarchy

d) direct democracy
e) constitutional monarchy
f) representative democracy

2.

a) True

b) False

c) True

d) False

e) True

f) False

(12)

3.

A state or society without a government

4.

Accept any reasonable response

5.

Accept any reasonable response

6.

A system of government in which voters choose representatives to act in their interests

7.

Possible answers:

a) United States

b) England

c) Cuba

(13)

1.

a) Miguel Hidalgo

b) September 16, 1810

c) federation

d) The Constitution of the United Mexican States

e) liberty

f) Mexico City

g) citizen

h) February 5, 1917

2.

a) 3

b) 5

c) 6

d) 2

d) 4

(14)

EZ✓

EZ✓

Freedom from Spain

(16)

1.

a) False – colony of Spain

b) False – September 16

c) True

d) True

2.

a) Mexico City

b) federation

c) Miguel Hidalgo

d) titles

(17)

3.

Freedom. Accept any reasonable response.

4.

Outlines rights and responsibilities of citizens, describes how the government should be run

5.

Fierce fighting about rights and equality

6.

executive, legislative, judicial

7.

Accept any verifiable answers

(18)

Accept any reasonable response

(20)

a) In any order: executive, legislative, judicial

b) legislative

c) president

d) Justices

e) executive

f) judicial

g) legislative

h) sexenio

(21)

1.

Executive: makes sure laws are obeyed, constitution is followed

Legislative: makes laws

Judicial: answers questions about meanings of laws

2.

Accept verifiable answers

(23)

1.

a) False – democracy would be best

b) True

c) False – very important

d) True

e) False – president

f) True

g) False – help the president

h) True

i) False – judicial branch

(24)

3.

a) O

b) F

c) O

d) O

e) F

f) O

g) O

h) F

i) O

j) O

4.

Accept most current information

(25)

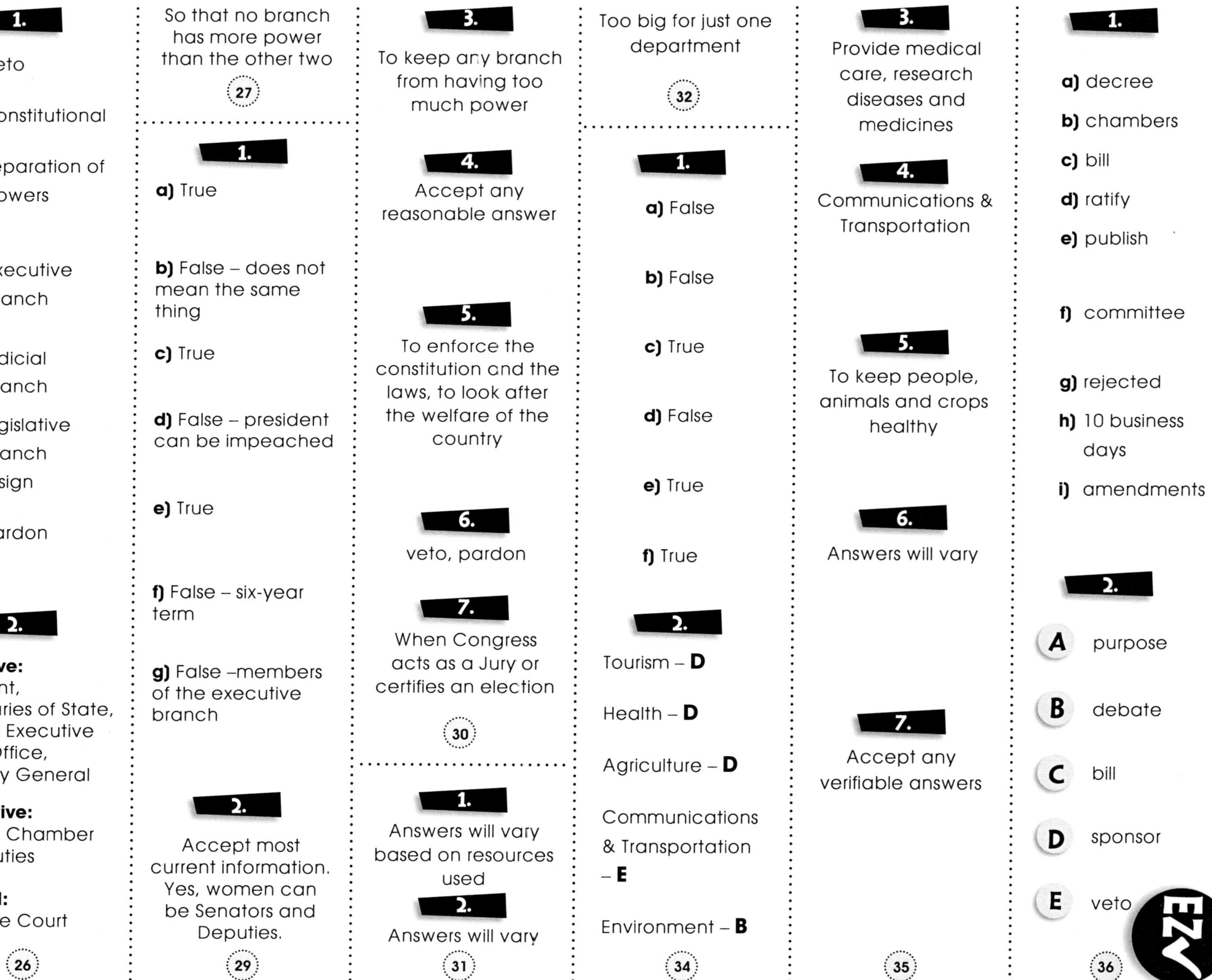

1.

a) veto

b) constitutional

c) separation of powers

d) executive branch

e) judicial branch

f) legislative branch

g) resign

h) pardon

2.

Executive: President, Secretaries of State, Federal Executive Legal Office, Attorney General

Legislative: Senate, Chamber of Deputies

Judicial: Supreme Court

26

So that no branch has more power than the other two

27

1.

a) True

b) False – does not mean the same thing

c) True

d) False – president can be impeached

e) True

f) False – six-year term

g) False –members of the executive branch

2.

Accept most current information. Yes, women can be Senators and Deputies.

29

3.

To keep any branch from having too much power

4.

Accept any reasonable answer

5.

To enforce the constitution and the laws, to look after the welfare of the country

6.

veto, pardon

7.

When Congress acts as a Jury or certifies an election

30

1.

Answers will vary based on resources used

2.

Answers will vary

31

Too big for just one department

32

1.

a) False

b) False

c) True

d) False

e) True

f) True

2.

Tourism – **D**

Health – **D**

Agriculture – **D**

Communications & Transportation – **E**

Environment – **B**

34

3.

Provide medical care, research diseases and medicines

4.

Communications & Transportation

5.

To keep people, animals and crops healthy

6.

Answers will vary

7.

Accept any verifiable answers

35

1.

a) decree

b) chambers

c) bill

d) ratify

e) publish

f) committee

g) rejected

h) 10 business days

i) amendments

2.

A purpose

B debate

C bill

D sponsor

E veto

36

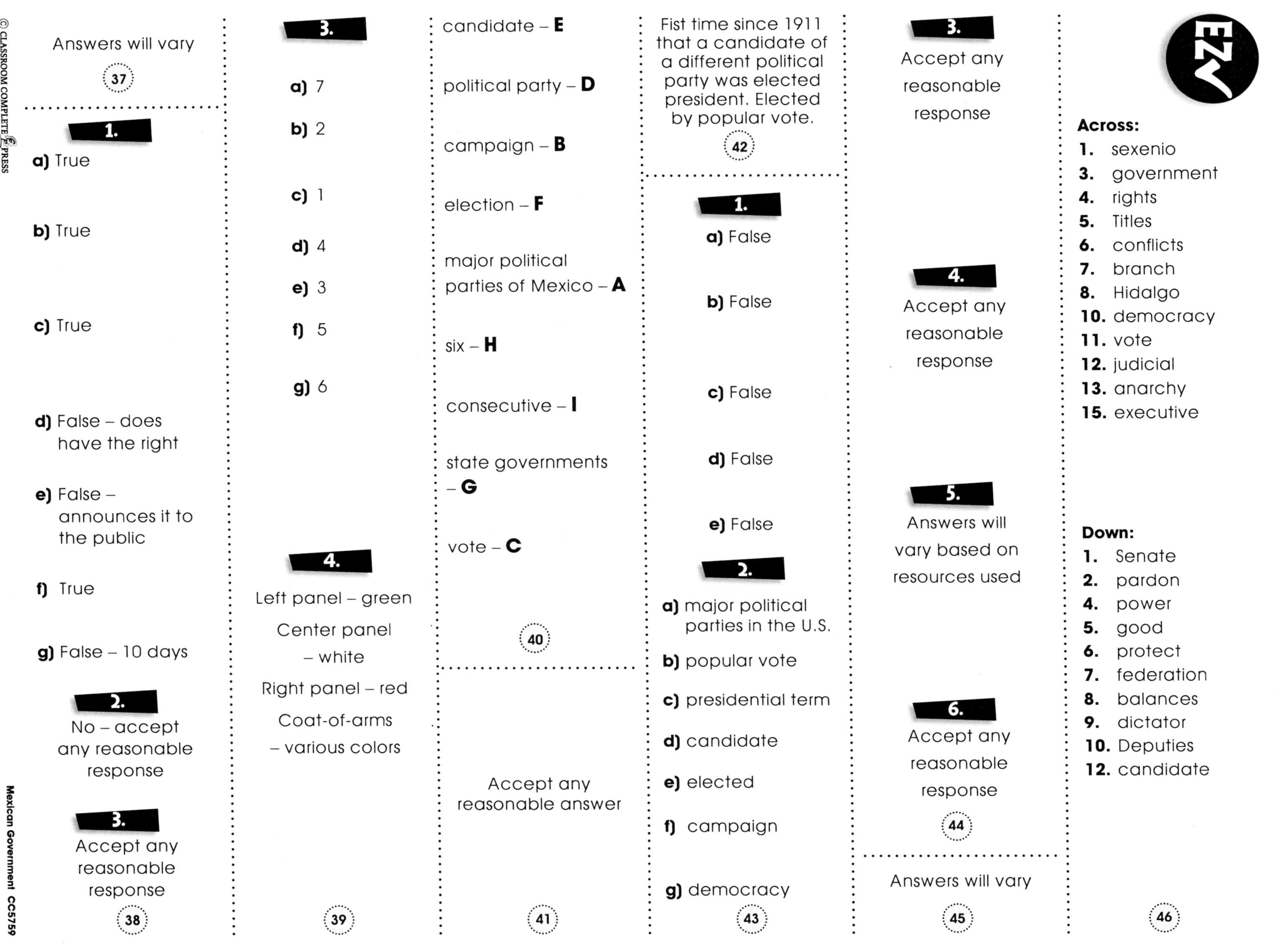

Answers will vary

(37)

1.

a) True

b) True

c) True

d) False – does have the right

e) False – announces it to the public

f) True

g) False – 10 days

2.

No – accept any reasonable response

3.

Accept any reasonable response

(38)

3.

a) 7

b) 2

c) 1

d) 4

e) 3

f) 5

g) 6

4.

Left panel – green

Center panel – white

Right panel – red

Coat-of-arms – various colors

(39)

candidate – **E**

political party – **D**

campaign – **B**

election – **F**

major political parties of Mexico – **A**

six – **H**

consecutive – **I**

state governments – **G**

vote – **C**

(40)

Accept any reasonable answer

(41)

Fist time since 1911 that a candidate of a different political party was elected president. Elected by popular vote.

(42)

1.

a) False

b) False

c) False

d) False

e) False

2.

a) major political parties in the U.S.

b) popular vote

c) presidential term

d) candidate

e) elected

f) campaign

g) democracy

(43)

3.

Accept any reasonable response

4.

Accept any reasonable response

5.

Answers will vary based on resources used

6.

Accept any reasonable response

(44)

Answers will vary

(45)

Across:

1. sexenio
3. government
4. rights
5. Titles
6. conflicts
7. branch
8. Hidalgo
10. democracy
11. vote
12. judicial
13. anarchy
15. executive

Down:

1. Senate
2. pardon
4. power
5. good
6. protect
7. federation
8. balances
9. dictator
10. Deputies
12. candidate

(46)

Word Search Answers

c	h	e	c	k	s	a	b	s	r	e	b	m	a	h	a	c	d
m	i	l	k	j	t	i	h	g	f	e	r	d	c	b	u	z	y
n	d	o	p	q	h	i	n	o	d	r	a	p	r	s	t	u	v
d	a	c	b	a	g	z	t	y	x	w	n	v	u	t	h	r	q
e	l	f	g	h	i	i	j	l	k	l	c	m	n	b	o	p	q
r	g	s	p	o	r	n	m	l	e	k	h	j	i	h	r	e	a
a	o	e	d	f	g	t	e	w	q	s	e	n	m	u	i	i	n
e	v	i	i	b	o	i	n	e	x	e	s	e	n	e	t	l	s
m	n	t	s	y	t	u	b	v	e	j	q	k	b	e	y	l	i
h	o	r	n	o	e	l	k	r	y	c	a	r	c	o	m	e	d
t	r	a	e	r	v	o	t	e	p	o	r	y	k	r	j	a	w
w	i	p	z	l	m	e	x	i	c	o	c	i	t	y	y	d	c
s	n	v	i	p	e	y	r	d	s	a	q	w	e	h	r	e	o
b	d	e	t	y	q	c	u	e	j	w	b	e	e	c	o	r	n
w	e	g	i	h	j	k	t	s	i	z	x	p	a	r	t	e	s
i	p	e	c	w	q	a	r	e	s	g	d	o	f	a	h	j	t
j	e	c	r	v	b	e	m	y	d	e	n	l	w	n	e	r	i
y	n	f	g	h	b	l	h	x	c	n	m	i	q	o	w	e	t
p	d	q	u	m	r	c	e	r	w	q	m	t	n	m	b	v	u
l	e	w	a	o	r	y	o	t	n	e	d	i	s	e	r	p	t
a	n	h	b	a	j	f	g	d	s	d	s	c	a	q	w	q	i
l	c	a	n	m	n	o	f	e	d	e	r	a	t	i	o	n	o
h	e	a	f	e	f	y	s	e	h	s	i	l	b	u	p	h	n

47

Part A

1. True

2. False – governments are necessary

3. False – most are democracies

4. True

5. True

6. True

7. False – representative democracy

8. False – three

9. False – Secretaries of State

10. False – President, deputies and senators of the Congress and the legislatures of the States

48

Part B

1. Accept any reasonable response

2. Accept any reasonable response

3. Accept any reasonable response

4. Executive – make sure the laws are followed
Legislative – makes the laws
Judicial – answers questions about the laws and the Constitution

5. His actions led to the first Mexican constitution

49

EZ✓

Maya Temple (Chichén Itzá, Mexico)

Mexico's National Flag

Palacio del Ayuntamiento
(Zocalo Plaza, Mexico City)

Political Map of Mexico

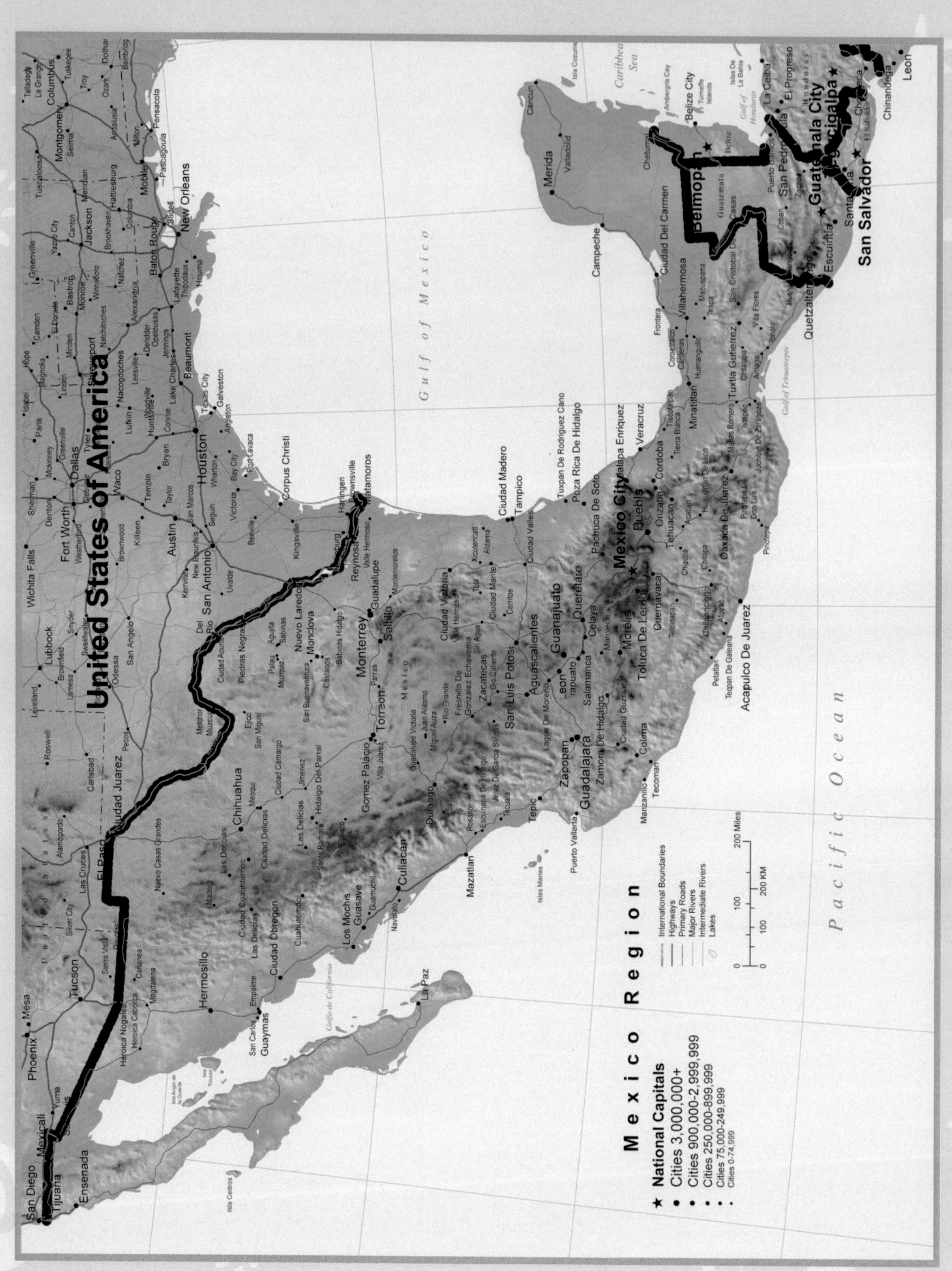

The Independence Angel
(a 1910 monument honoring Mexico's independence)

Currency of Mexico